ART DECO
JEWELRY DESIGNS

ART DECO JEWELRY DESIGNS

in Full Color

Idées-Paris

DOVER PUBLICATIONS, INC.
New York

Copyright © 1993 by Dover Publications, Inc.

Published in Canada by General Publishing Company, Ltd., 30 Lesmill Road, Don Mills, Toronto, Ontario.

Published in the United Kingdom by Constable and Company, Ltd., 3 The Lanchesters, 162–164 Fulham Palace Road, London W6 9ER.

This Dover edition, first published in 1993, contains all 36 plates and the inside back cover illustration originally published as *Le plus bel album du monde pour les industries de luxe*, Idées-Paris, Paris, n.d. See the new Publisher's Note for further details.

DOVER *Pictorial Archive* SERIES

Manufactured in the United States of America
Dover Publications, Inc., 31 East 2nd Street, Mineola, N.Y. 11501

Library of Congress Cataloging-in-Publication Data

Plus bel album du monde pour les industries de luxe. English.
    Art deco·jewelry designs in full color / Idées-Paris.
        p.   cm.—(Dover pictorial archive series)
    Translation of: Le plus bel album du monde pour les industries de luxe.
    ISBN 0-486-27694-5 (pbk.)
    1. Idées-Paris (Firm)—Themes, motives. 2. Jewelry—France—History—20th century—Themes, motives. 3. Decoration and ornament—France—Art deco. I. Idées-Paris (Firm)
II. Title. III. Series.
NK7398.I34A4   1993
745.4'4944361'09041—dc20
                                                                       93-10730
                                                                      CIP

PUBLISHER'S NOTE

I N THE FIRST FOUR DECADES of this century, Paris reigned supreme as the undisputed arbiter of style in the lapidary arts. Eminent design studios created exciting new patterns for *les industries de luxe:* jewelry making, engraving and fashion design. Art publishers issued a stream of stimulating portfolios. The useful and the beautiful were indissolubly wedded.

The present volume reproduces all 36 plates from *Le plus bel album du monde pour les industries de luxe,* produced by the *atelier* Idées-Paris. The plates illustrate the scope of decorative versatility in Art Deco jewelry. Dozens of beautiful designs, representing the cutting edge of late-Twenties Paris fashion, are shown in lavish detail. Striking yet exquisite colors, combined with freely flowing forms, result in a group of designs that are ideally representative of their day and look boldly forward to the art of the Thirties.

The portfolio itself was apparently intended as an advertisement for the design services of Idées-Paris. A promotional notice exhorted customers not satisfied with the portfolio's wealth of images to forward their own "detailed indications" for jewelry designs to the studio, at which point Idées-Paris' "special artistic designer will then work out the desired sketch." Customers who wished to place substantial orders for the manufacture of a design were advised to utilize the services of Dirschmidt & Wagner, jewelers of Gablonz [Jablonec], Czechoslovakia, "which make a specialty of the manufacture of high-grade jewel-stone." Not surprisingly, a full-page advertisement for Dirschmidt & Wagner appeared on the inside back cover of *Le plus bel album du monde pour les industries de luxe.* It is duly reproduced in the present volume.

The portfolio's original introductory notes, which appeared in French, German, Spanish and English, colorfully describe, to what must have been an international audience, the Paris fashions of the day as reflected in the plates. The following is an edited version of those notes:

Jewelry. Dog collars will be the fashion for important evenings; they will be 1.5 to 3 cm high. Colored stones will be used only here and there; baguettes will frequently be worn, as before.

Clips. They hold their own and are much appreciated as brooches for dresses; some even have a pendant, which is the latest fashion. Some of them are very original and fanciful in design: dog's heads, butterflies, little watches, flowers. For men, little clips with decoration of enamel or monogram, about 1 inch wide, affixed to the thin watch chain, are the latest in waistcoat-pocket fashion.

Bracelets are much wider, as are the "slave rings" or "snakes."

Cut stones. They are preferred where there is not enough room to work the metal. . . . Instead of stones (such as lapis lazuli, onyx, coral and jade), stone-shaped, mat-polished platinum, bordered with discreet designs, can be used. These platinum shapes can also be bordered with enamel stripes.

Tiepins. Small fancies, baguettes only. Ladies also use them as decorative pins.

Wristwatches. For ladies only, fashionable in the shape called "elongated baguette," in dyed metal of different tints. For men, the watch should be plain and severe, owing to the "sports fashion," and worn on a chain; also, a wristwatch that opens is being pushed.

Signet rings. Plain modern stones or engraved, in all colors; also in enamel or metal in different tints.

Imitation. Fantasy plays a greater part here, although Paris has created numerous fantasy articles in real jewelry. The stones cut and used for brooches, clips, rings, etc., are much larger. . . . Chokers and sautoirs are long and of one color if possible (crystal) for evening wear. For day use, plain ones, especially turquoise, or bicolored ones, chiefly black and white or topaz-coral, are preferred. Metal alloys are used very little or not at all.

In all branches, great attention has to be paid today to the stones, which must be modern in both cutting and engraving.

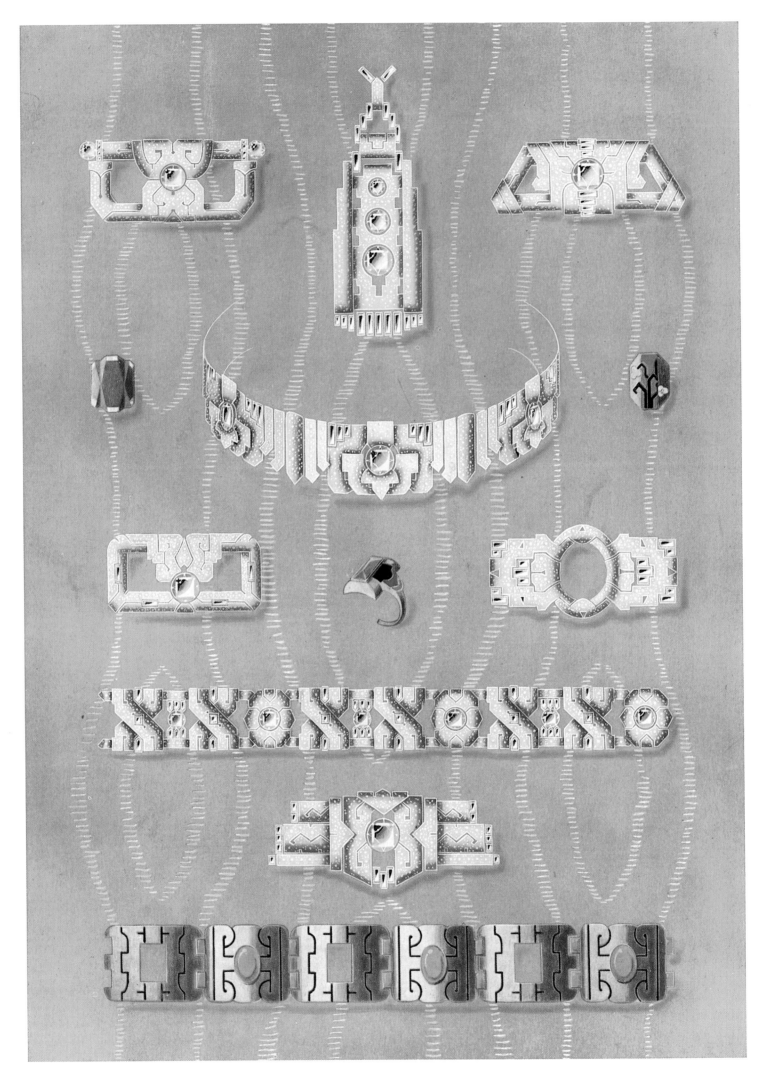

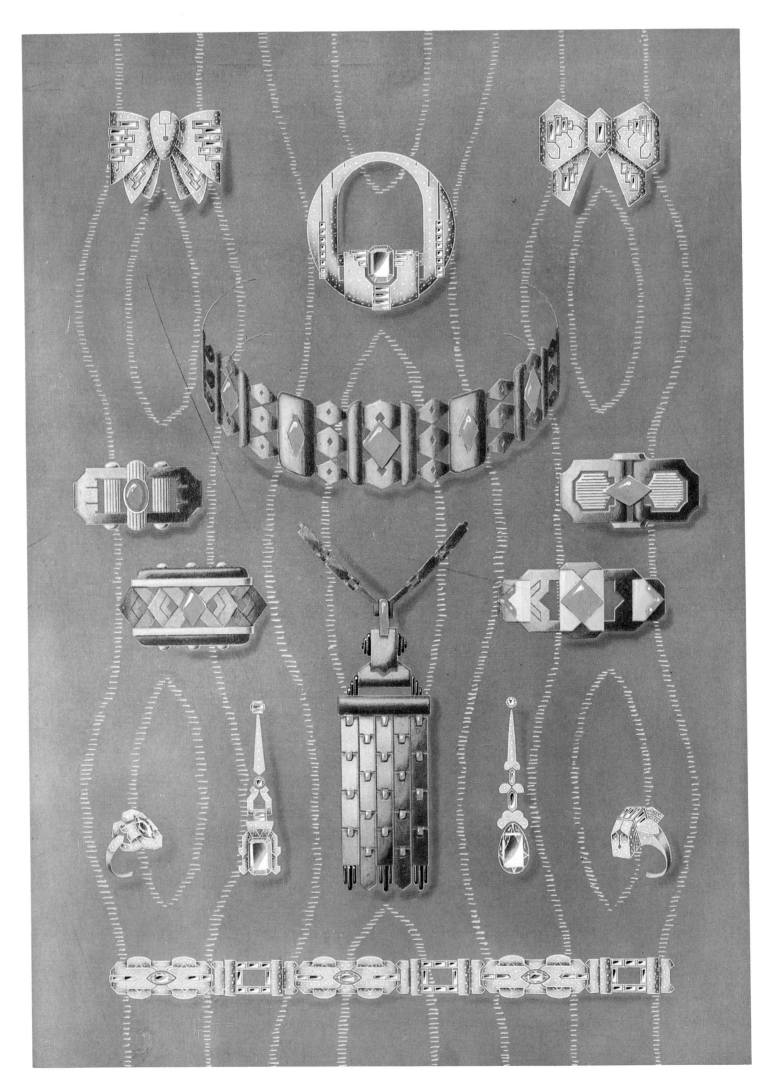

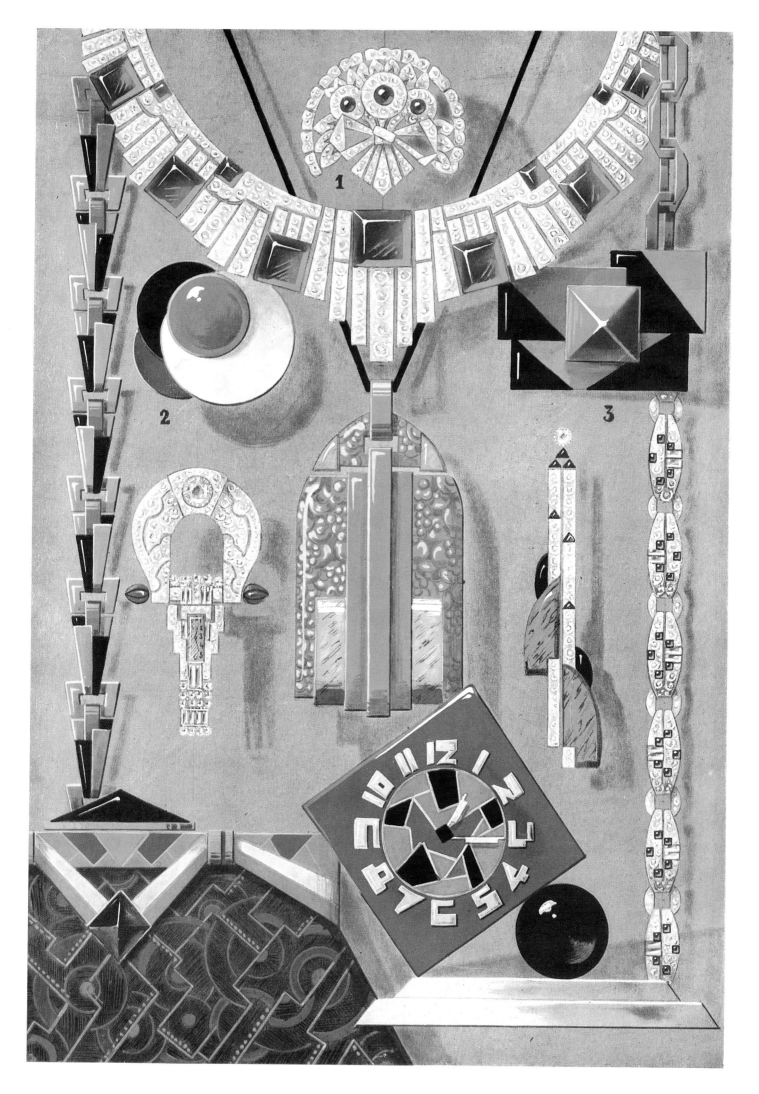

5

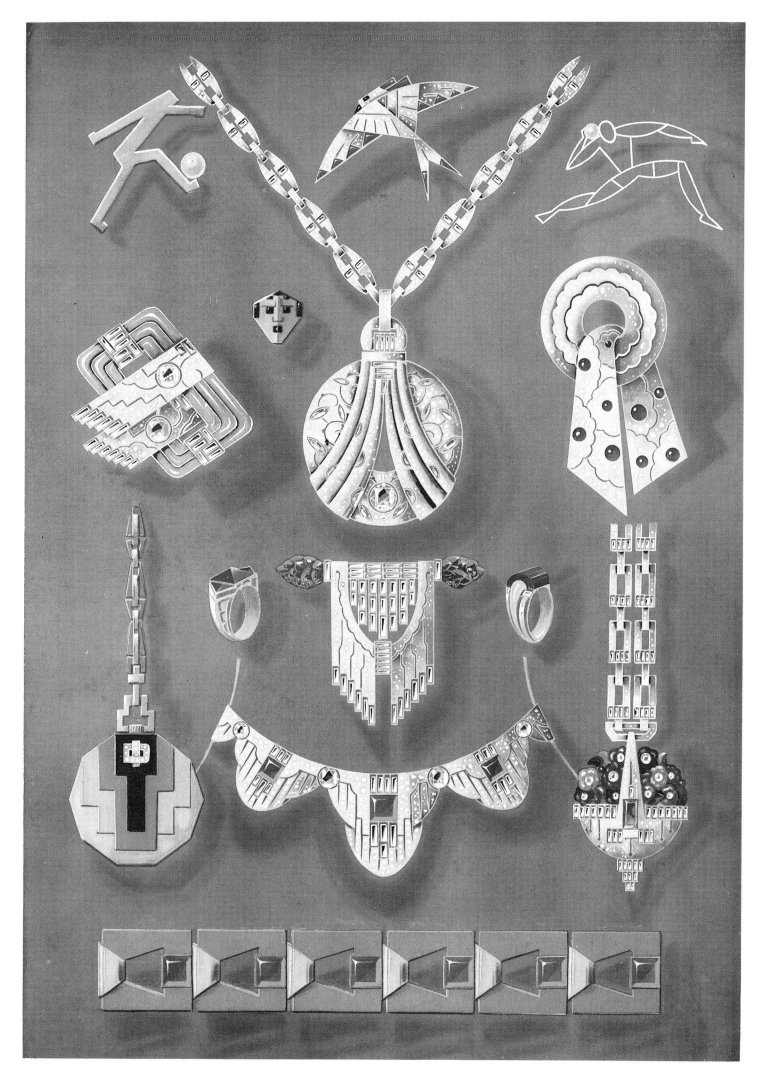

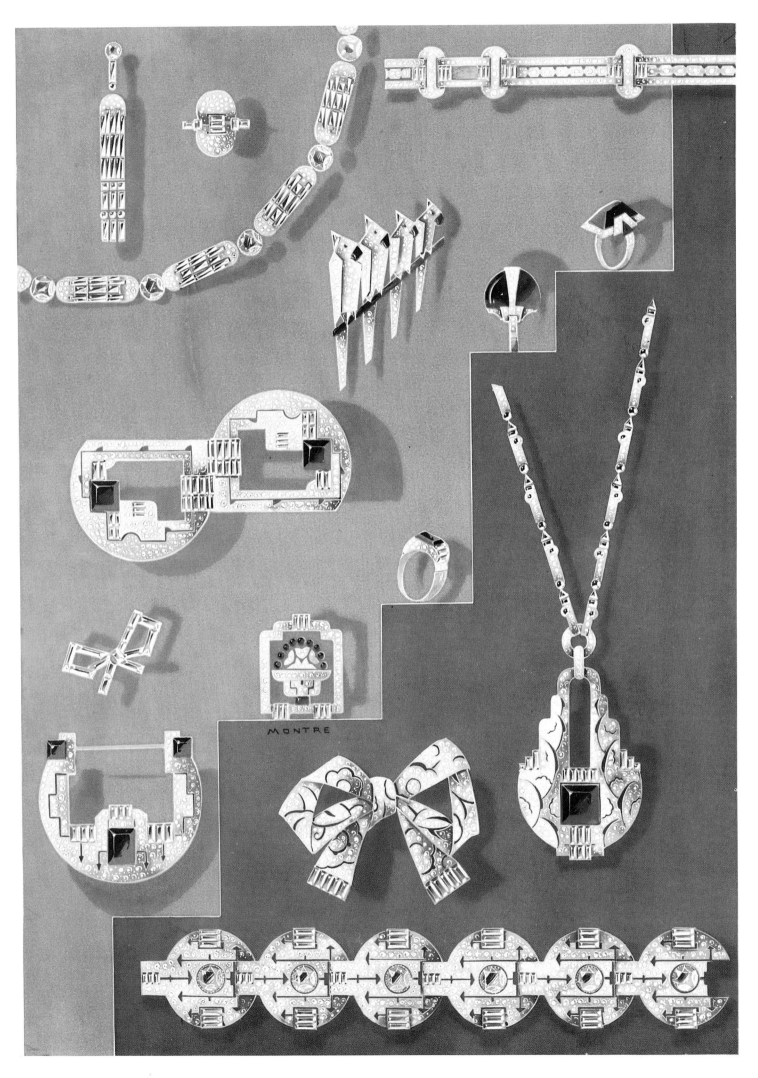

MONTRE

Cendrier
aschenbecher
ash-pan

IDÉES PARIS.

5.

10

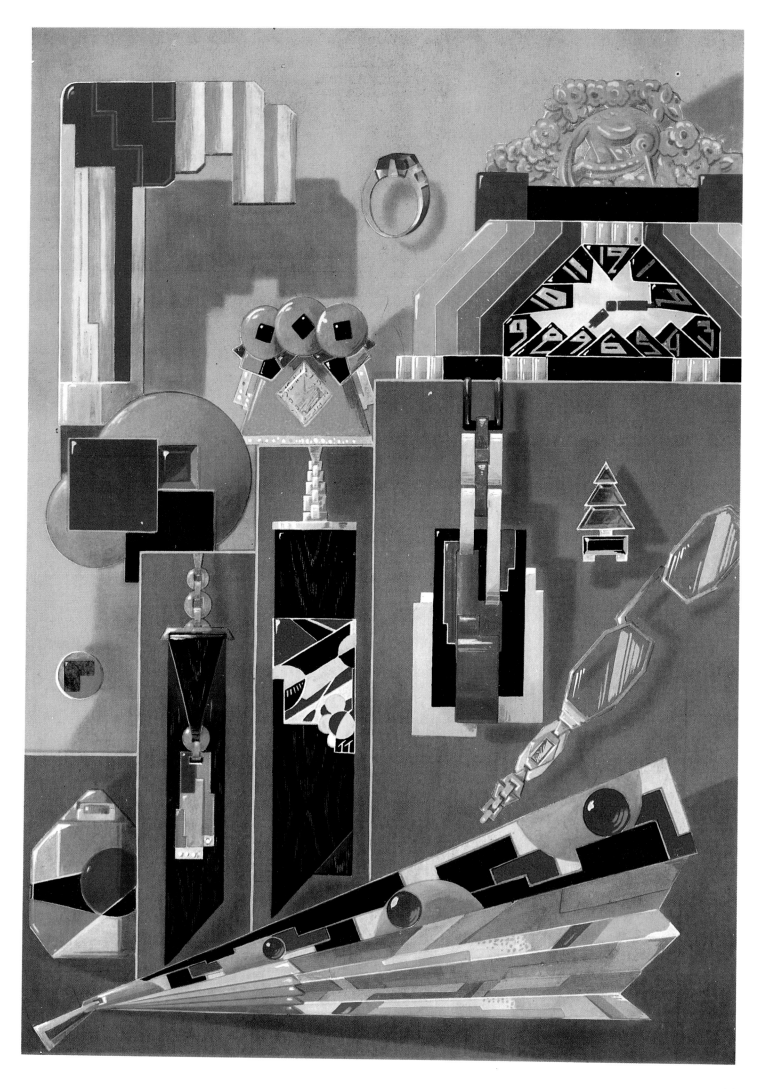

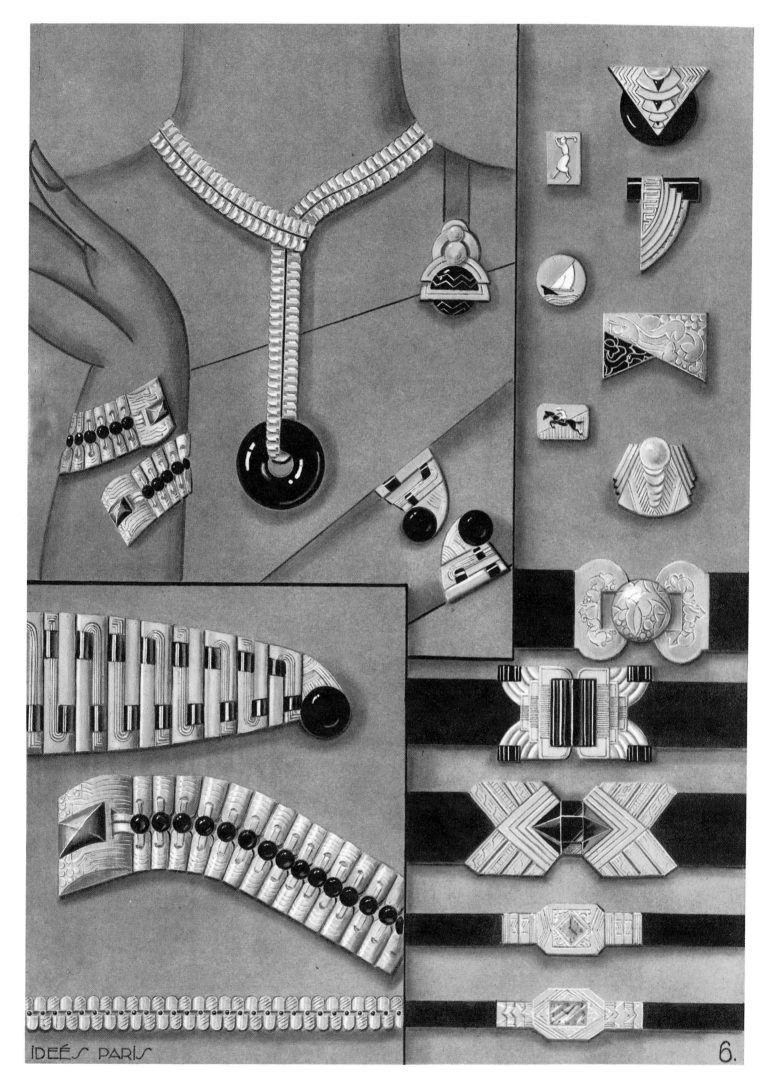

IDEÉS PARIS

6.

13

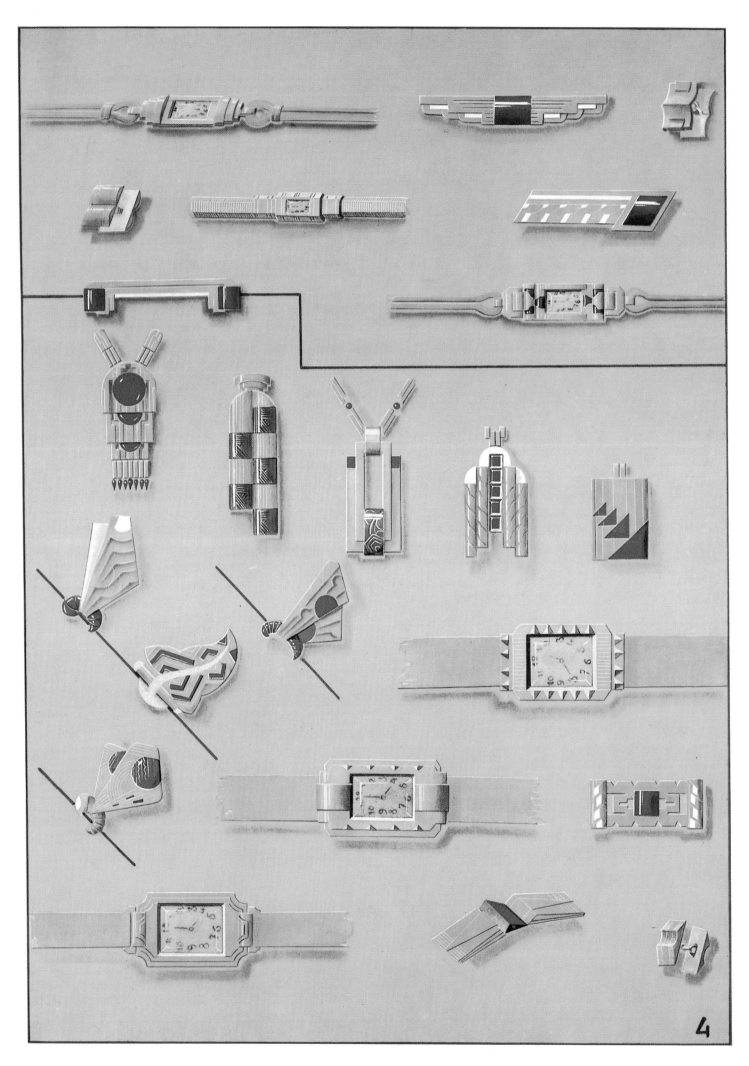

4

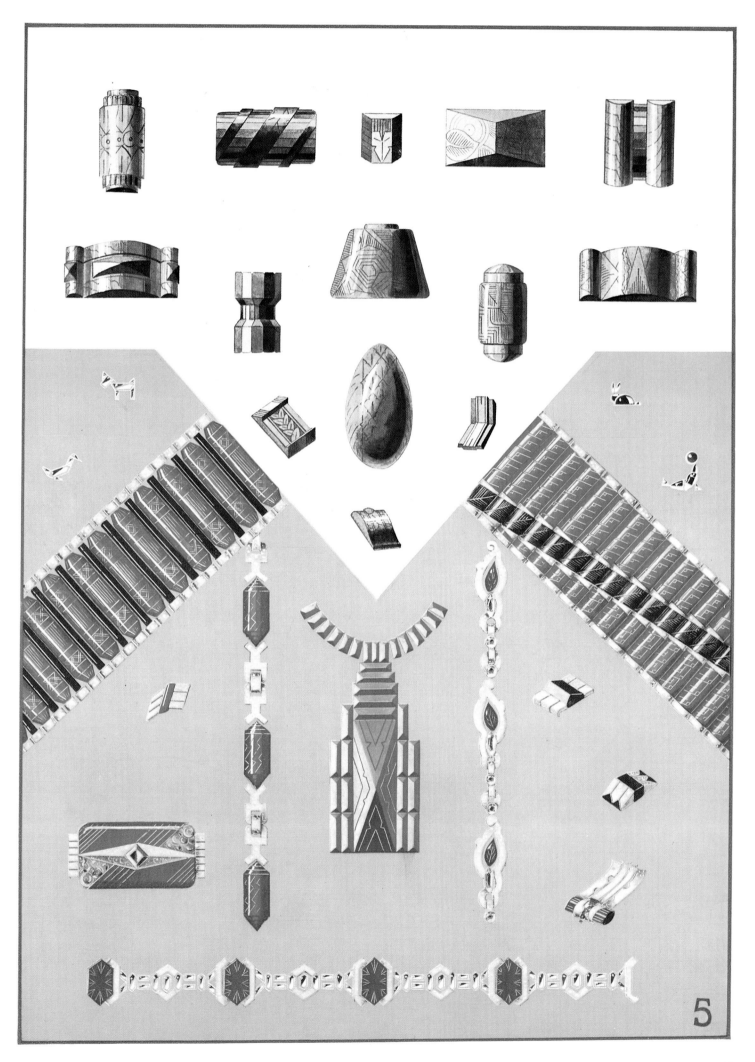

5

15

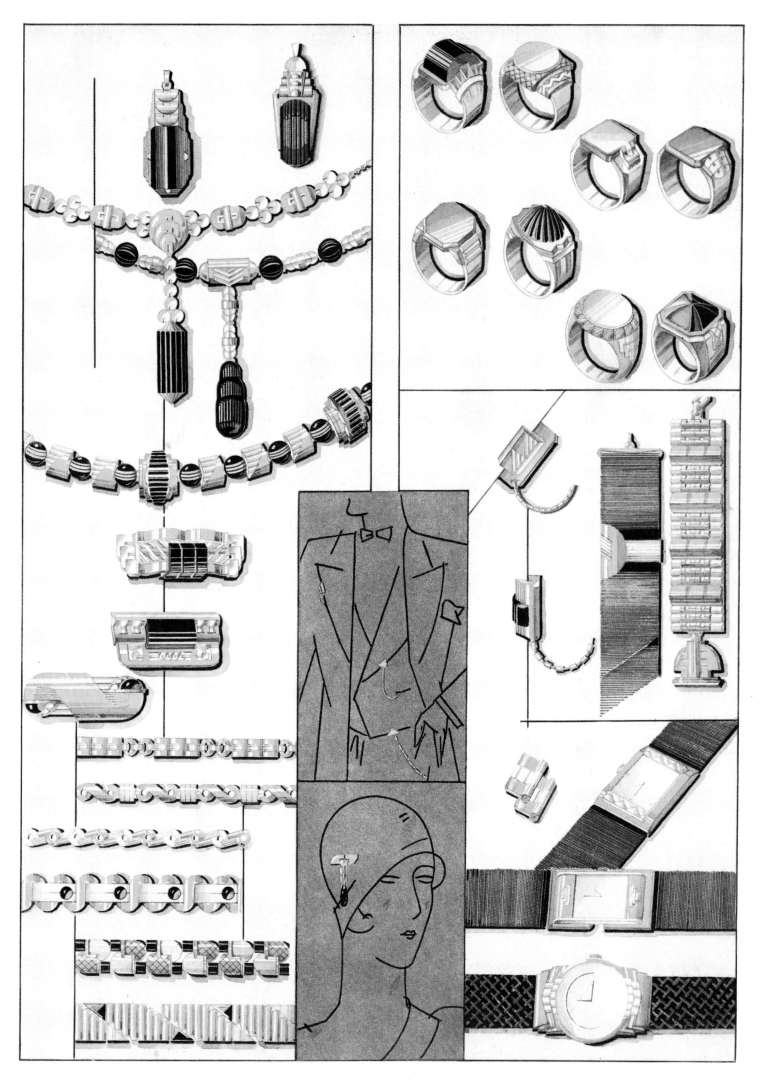

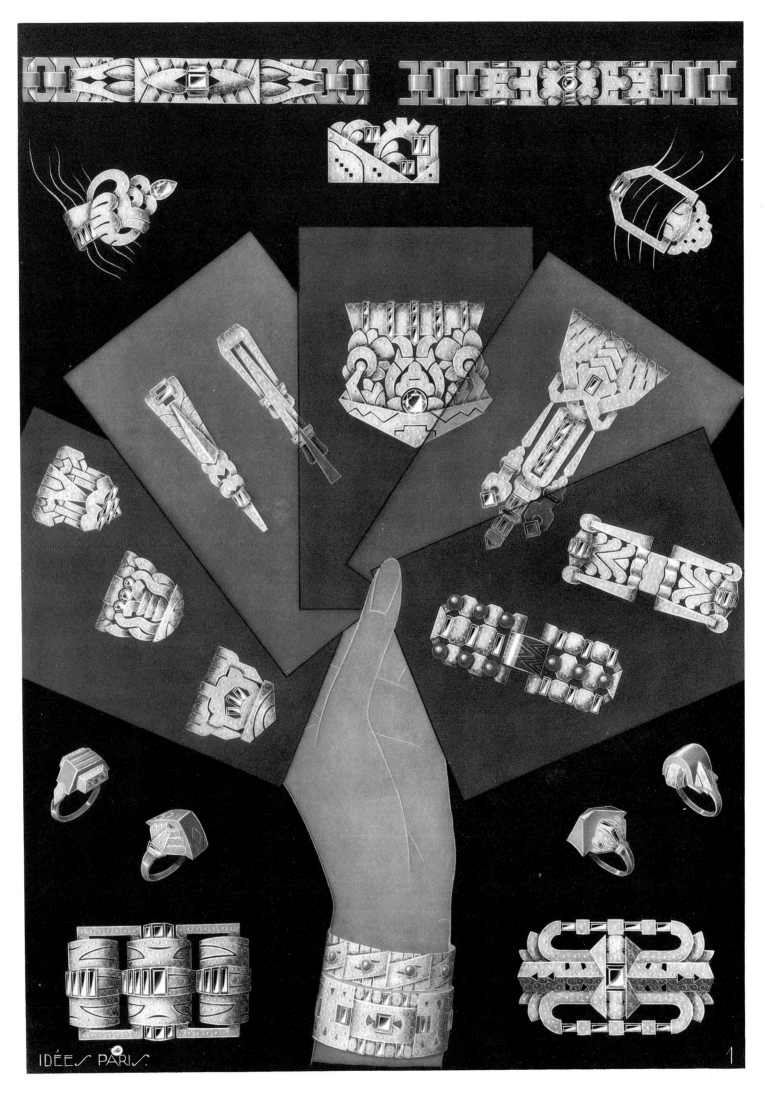

1

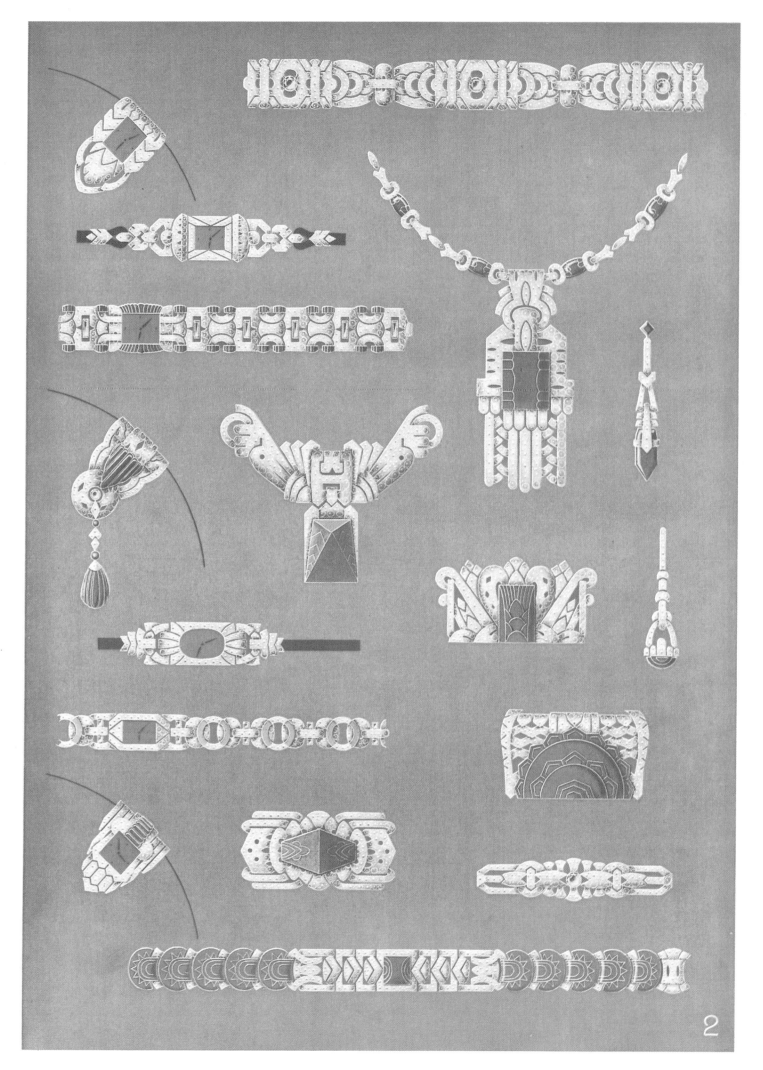

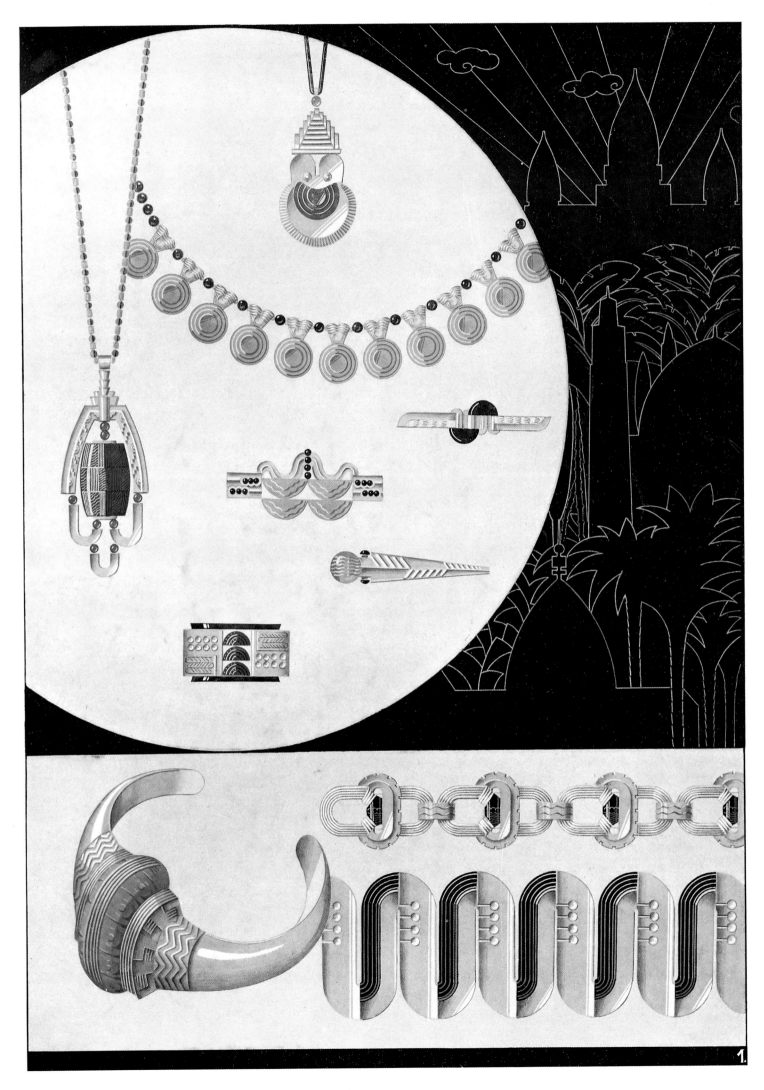

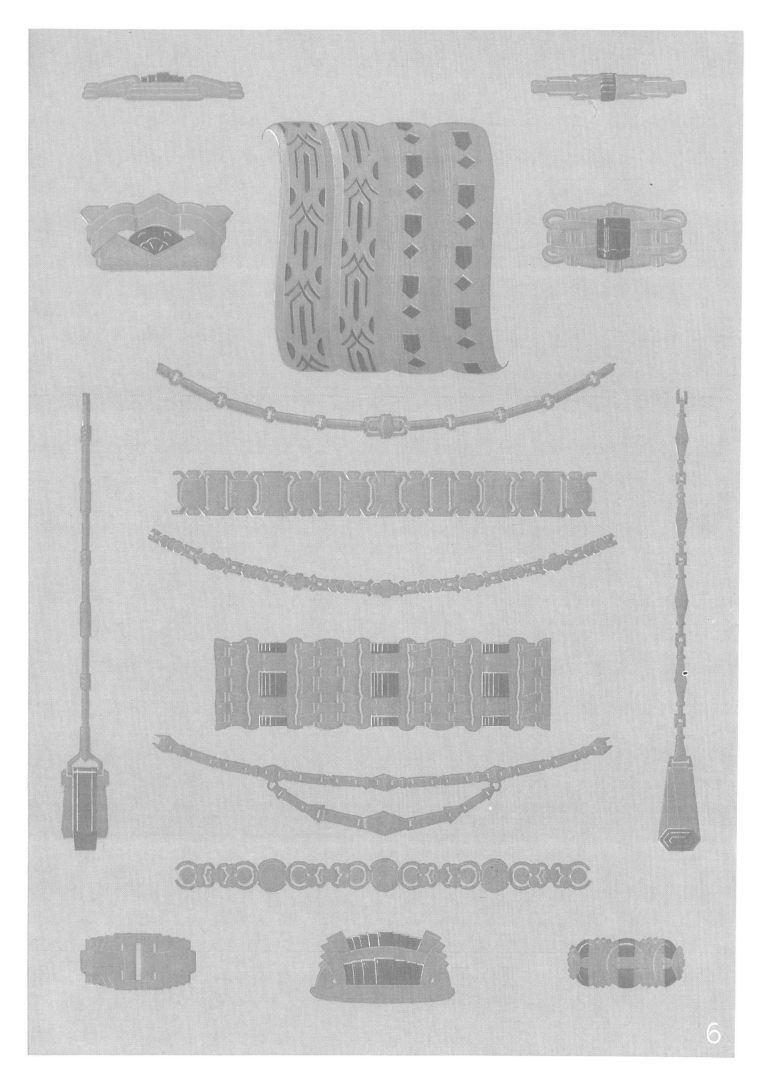

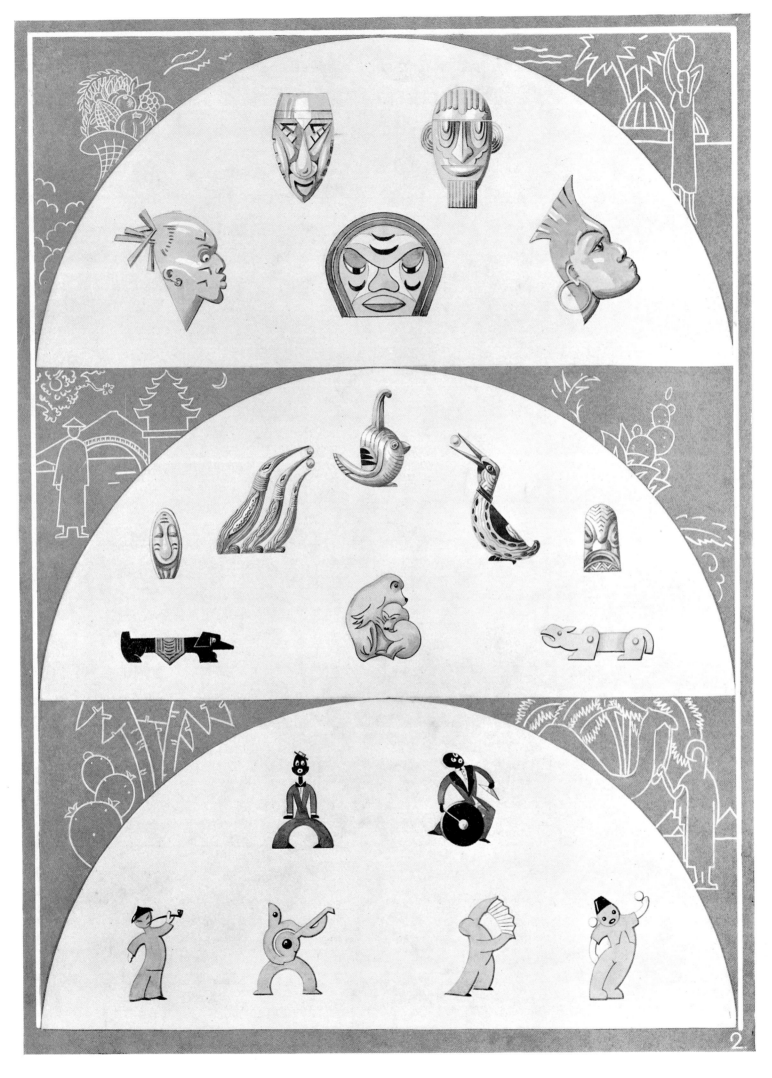

PRISTAL

LA GRANDE MODE

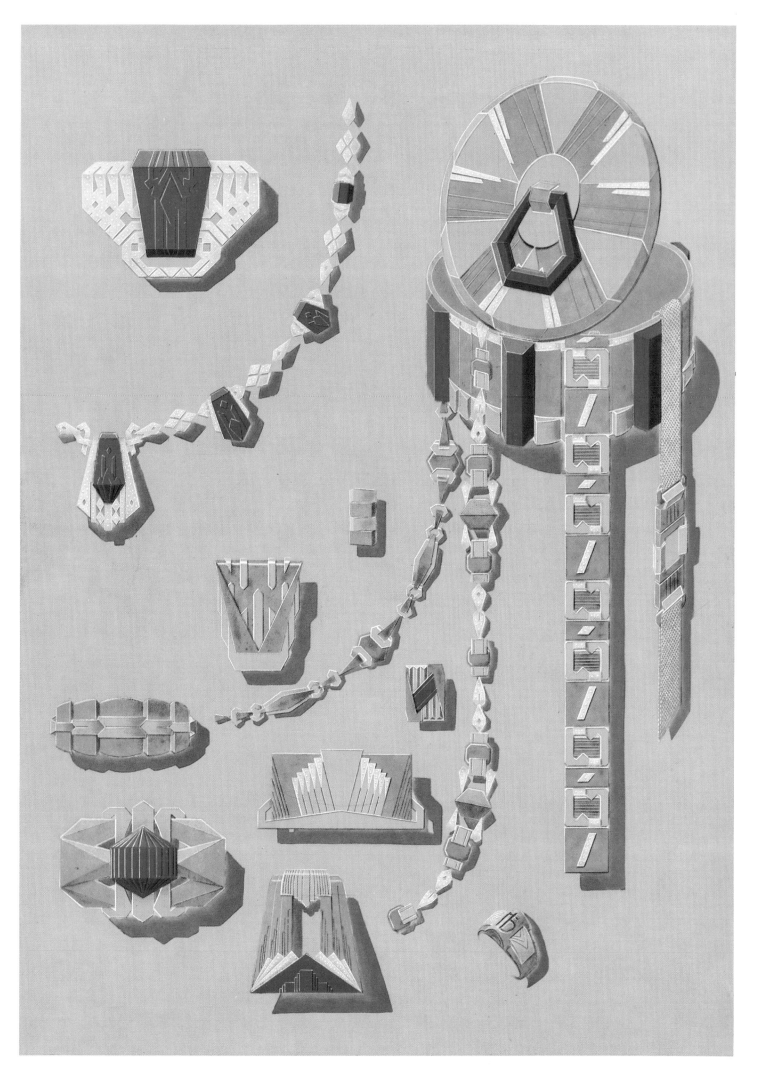

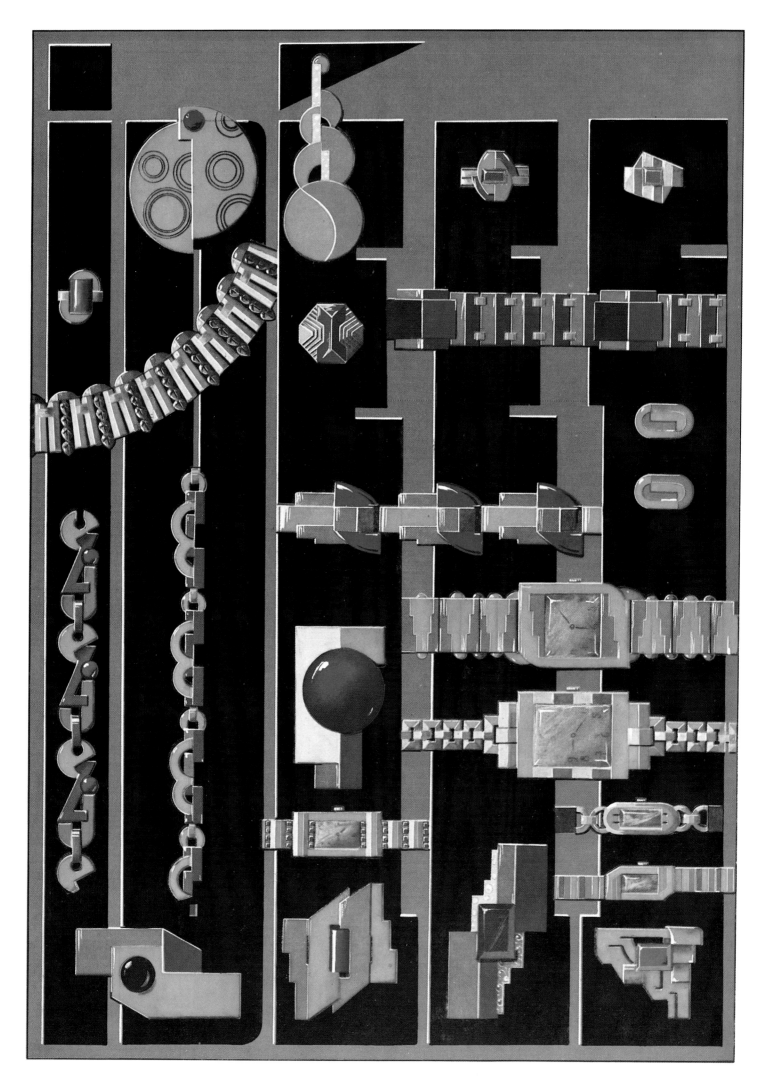

29

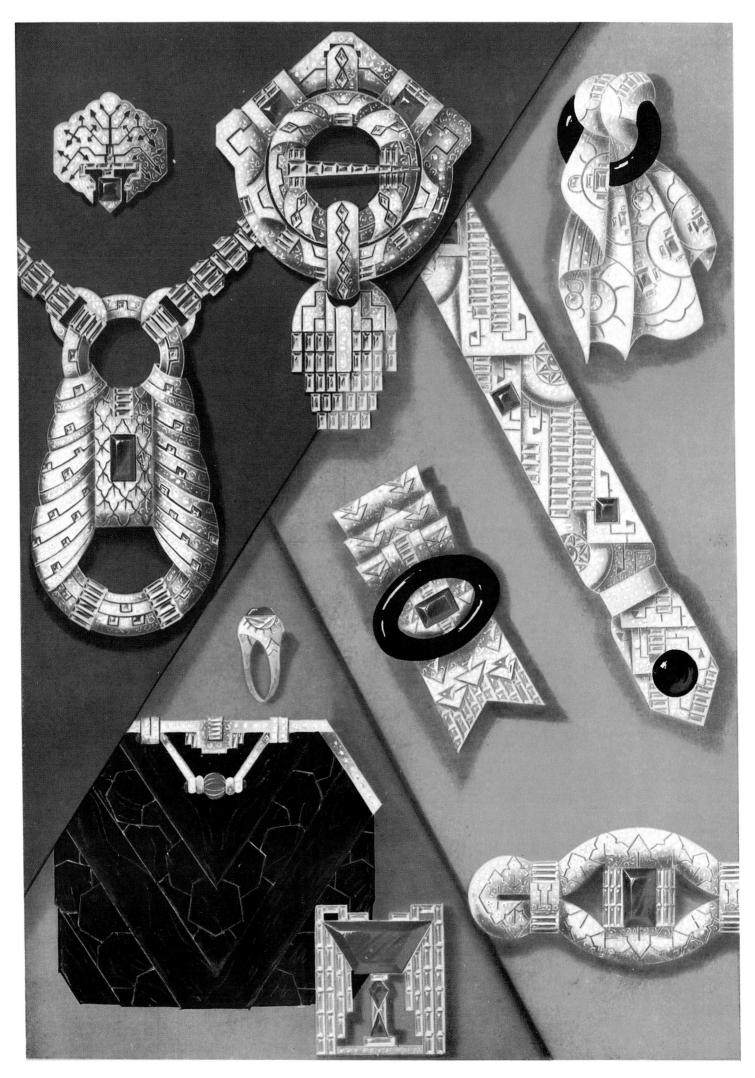

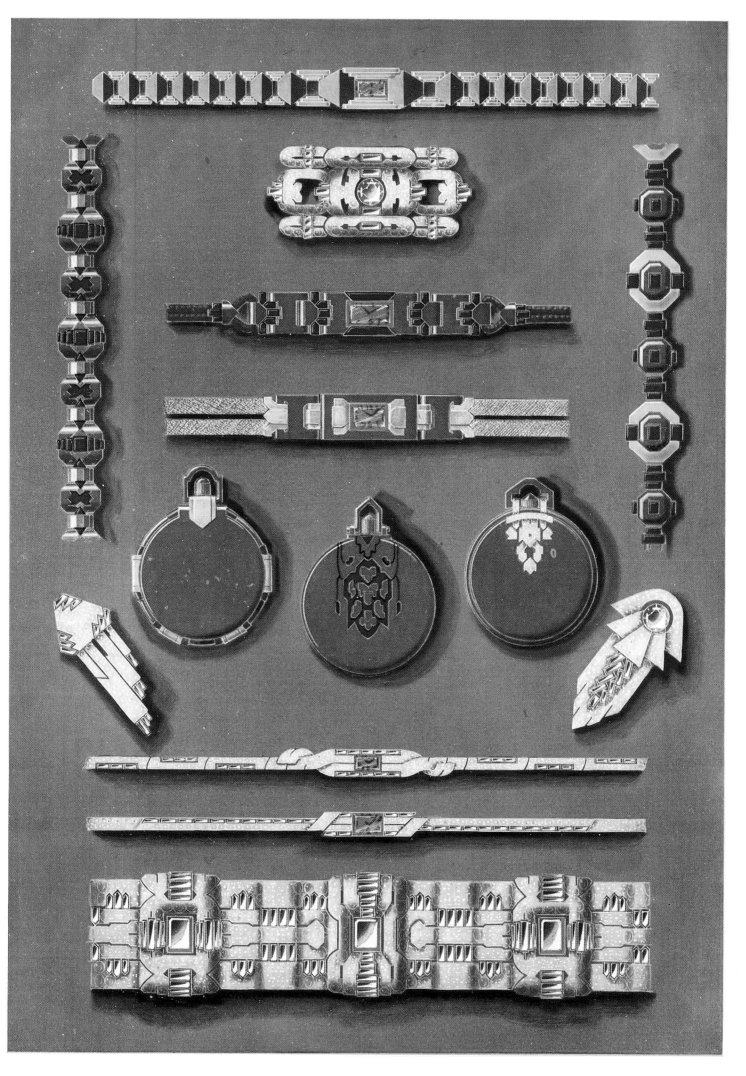

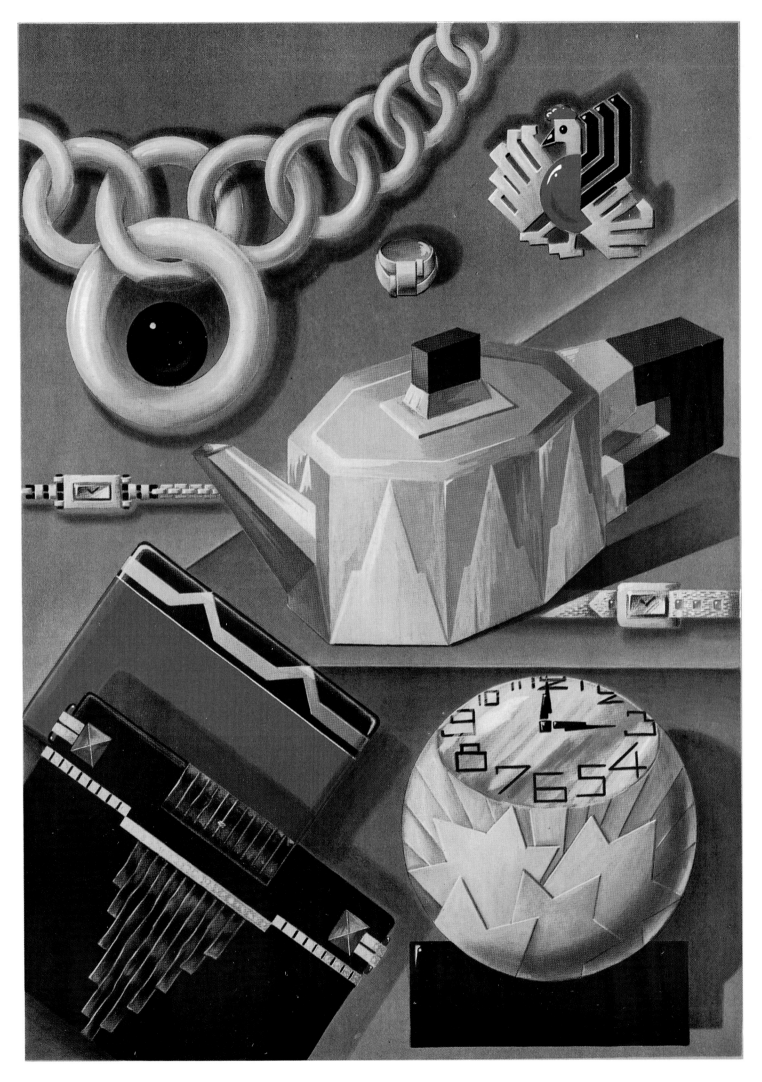

35

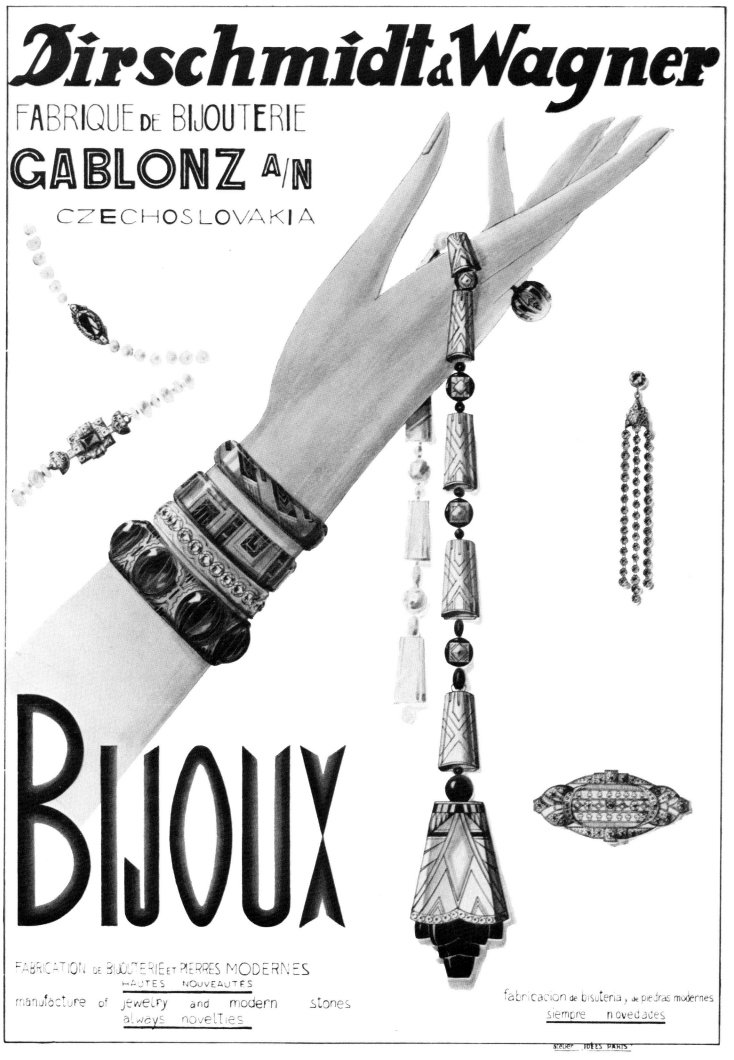

Dirschmidt & Wagner

FABRIQUE DE BIJOUTERIE

GABLONZ A/N

CZECHOSLOVAKIA

BIJOUX

37